HORRIBLE JOBS OF THE

INDUSTRIAL REVOLUTION

Gareth Stevens
Publishing

LEON GRAY

Please visit our website, www.garethstevens.com.
For a free color catalog of all our high-quality books,
call toll free 1-800-542-2595 or fax 1-877-542-2596.

Library of Congress Cataloging-in-Publication Data

Gray, Leon.
Horrible jobs of the Industrial Revolution / by Leon Gray.
    p. cm. — (History's most horrible jobs)
Includes index.
ISBN 978-1-4824-0344-2 (pbk.)
ISBN 978-1-4824-3307-4 (6-pack)
ISBN 978-1-4824-0343-5 (library binding)
1. Industrial revolution — Juvenile literature. 2. Industrial revolution — England — History –
Juvenile literature. 3. Industrial revolution — United States — History — Juvenile literature. I.
Gray, Leon, 1974-. II. Title.
HC51.G73 2014
909.81—dc23

First Edition

Published in 2014 by
Gareth Stevens Publishing
111 East 14th Street, Suite 349
New York, NY 10003

© 2014 Gareth Stevens Publishing

Produced by Calcium, www.calciumcreative.co.uk
Designed by Simon Borrough
Edited by Sarah Eason and Rachel Blount

Cover Illustration by Jim Mitchell

Photo credits: Dreamstime: Christianm 27b, Denisnata 19, Dja65 7t, Dvmsimages 37t, 39t,
39cr, Marilyngould 44, Markwr 6, Rvlsoft 45, Ryme 37b, Skypixel 14; Flickr: Brizzle born and
bred 18; Getty Images: 17; Library of Congress: George Grantham Bain Collection 21, Lewis
Wickes Hine 10, 23, Andrew J. Russell 34; Shutterstock: 1000 Words 38, Antonio Abrignani
8, 11, 43, Amenhotepov 35l, Anneka 35tl, Anyaivanova 5, Laurie Barr 25b, Catwalker 12,
Chiyacat 24c, CRM 33, Fer Gregory 35r, Jamesdavidphoto 31, KariDesign 39b, Gary Paul
Lewis 25t, Lineartestpilot 24b, Morphart Creation 13, 16, Olmarmar 9, Vladimir Salman
41t, Richard Semik 20, Winai Tepsuttinun 32b, Varbenov 22r, Villorejo 7b; Nigel Wilkes 30;
Wikimedia Commons: Baines 22l, William Hogarth, The Yorck Project 36, Henry Mayhew
40, Henry Mayhew / John Binny 27t, Henry Mayhew / William Tuckniss 41b, Mtaylor848 29,
Mussklprozz 32t, Gerald Palmer 4, Quaziefoto 15, Darren Wyn Rees 28, John Savage 26.

Printed in the United States of America.

CPSIA compliance information: Batch #CW14GS: For further information contact Gareth Stevens, New York, New York at 1-800-542-2595.

Contents

Chapter One
Down the Mine

Between 1750 and the mid-to-late 1800s, there was an Industrial Revolution in Europe and the United States. Before this time, most people lived in the country and farmed the land. By the end of the Industrial Revolution, many people lived in the towns around coal mines or moved to big cities to work in factories.

This image shows coal miners leaving a mine in northern England at the end of another long shift of underground work.

Fuel for Thought

Coal was the fuel of the Industrial Revolution. Machines such as steam engines and blast furnaces burned coal for power. Steam engines needed a lot of coal to heat water to turn it into steam. The hot steam pushed and pulled pistons that turned wheels to generate power.

Deep Underground

The problem with coal was that it was buried deep underground. That meant someone had to dig it out. This was a dangerous and horrible job. Entire families worked in mines—even children as young as 6 years old were employed.

Extracting Iron

In 1709, Abraham Darby built a coal-powered blast furnace to extract iron from its ore. Ore is rock that contains metal. During the Industrial Revolution, there was a great demand for iron. It was used to build bridges, machines, ships, trains, and weapons.

Coke

Before Darby built his blast furnace, iron was expensive because it was hard to extract from its ore. Darby developed an efficient method of extracting iron using coke. Coke is a powdery form of coal that can melt ore, so that the iron can be extracted.

During the Industrial Revolution, coal was the fuel for enormous machines, such as this German steam train.

Coal Miner

Coal miners had to face many dangers every single day they went to work. They worked underground in near darkness, surrounded by poisonous fumes, with the constant threat that the mine they were working in might collapse. It was scary, dirty work.

The Coal Mine

Most coal deposits are buried deep underground. To reach the coal, miners dug a shaft straight down into the ground. They then dug tunnels leading off from the main mineshaft. Coal is found in layers between rock, and tunnels were dug to follow the seams of coal. The miners took an elevator down to the tunnels, and hacked at the coal using hand picks.

Getters and Putters

The miners who dug the coal were called "getters" and those who moved the coal to the surface were called "putters." Miners were allowed only short breaks and the work was very hard. The coal miners had to carry any food and drink they needed throughout the day with them, so it often got covered in coal dust.

Coal miners worked many miles under the ground in dark, cramped conditions.

Dangerous Work

Until safety lamps were invented, "getters" used candles to light dark tunnels. Explosions were a constant threat—as the miners dug deeper, they reached areas where dangerous gases had built up. A single spark from a pickax or a flicker from a candle could set these gases alight and cause an enormous explosion. The tunnels in the mines were held up only by wooden props, which often collapsed under the enormous weight of earth above them. Miners faced many other dangers, too, such as flooding and breathing in deadly coal dust. Miners were often sick and many died young.

The invention of the safety lamp made working in a coal mine much safer.

Coal miners used a hand pick such as this one to break coal from the seam.

A New Law

In 1842, the British government passed the Mines Act. This new law stopped boys under the age of 10 from working in the mines. The law also stopped women from working underground. This made many women angry because they lost their jobs in the mines and found it difficult to find other work.

Coal Hurrier

Another dangerous job in the coal mine was the coal hurrier. Often, the hurrier was the mother or the eldest child in a family. Hurriers pulled the heavy cartloads of coal through dark tunnels to the surface of the mine.

Tunnel Rats

The hurrier dragged the carts of coal using a chain, which clipped onto a leather belt around their waist. The hurrier clambered their way through a maze of tiny tunnels that were often full of dust, gas, and water. Many hurriers suffered back injuries and deformities from the constant heaving and stooping.

Hurriers worked on their hands and feet, dragging cartloads of coal along tunnels to the surface of the mine.

Coal is buried deep beneath the ground in layers called seams.

Chain Gang

Some hurriers worked in pairs, with one pulling and the other pushing the heavy carts through the narrow tunnels. The pusher was called a "thruster." The thrusters often used their heads to push the carts, which eventually made their hair fall out completely.

Mining in the United States

In the United States, coal mining mainly took place in Ohio, the Appalachian Mountains, Wyoming, northern Maryland, West Virginia, and Pennsylvania. Like children in Britain, young boys carried out backbreaking work in dangerous and horrible conditions.

Coal Trapper

Some children worked in the mines as coal "trappers." They opened and closed doors in the tunnels to let coal trucks through. This was an important job because it helped to ventilate the tunnels and kept explosive gases from building up in the mine.

A coal trapper had one of the loneliest jobs in the coal mine.

In the Dark

Trappers worked for up to 12 hours a day in total darkness, with only rats for company. Candles were expensive, and the flames were dangerous when mixed with explosive gases deep underground. One young boy who worked as a trapper said, "I sit in the dark down in the pit for 12 hours a day. I only see daylight on Sundays, when I don't work down the pit. Once I fell asleep and a wagon ran over my leg."

Moving On

Children carried out the horrible job of trapper until they were old and strong enough to push and pull the trucks, which were called "corfs." The youngest children who worked as trappers were just 5 years old.

THE HORRIBLE TRUTH

One day in 1838, it started to rain heavily at the Huskar coal mine in Silkstone, England. A local stream began to overflow into a ventilation shaft. Many children who were working in the mine became trapped by the floodwater. In total, 26 children between the ages of 8 and 15 died.

This young trapper is opening his trap door to let hurriers pushing a cartload of coal through the tunnel.

Chapter Two
Factory Workers

The Industrial Revolution changed the way people lived and worked. New machines were invented to speed up the process of making goods such as cotton thread, glassware, and soap. Huge factories were built in towns, and many people left the countryside to work in these industrial centers.

Town Jobs

Before factories, manufacturing items like cotton thread and soap was a small-scale operation carried out in the home by families. Machines in factories could do the work faster and more efficiently. As a result, if people wanted work, they had to move to towns to find work in the factories.

Cotton and Wool

Two important industries were cotton and wool manufacture. Machines spun cotton and wool into thread, which was turned into cloth. Factory owners built houses for workers near the factories, but the living conditions were poor. There was no running water and no toilets, so many people caught diseases and died young.

This photograph shows 12-year-old Addie Card, who worked at a cotton mill in 1912. The photo appeared on a stamp in 1998 to commemorate legal changes to child labor.

Noisy Towns

Factories were noisy places. Workers had to shout above the rattle and hiss of the machinery. The air was full of dust, fumes, and soot, so breathing was difficult. Iron and steel works were incredibly hot, and workers dripped with sweat. Smoke and smog billowed out into the air from the chimneys of the busy factories, and sparks and flames lit up the skies at night.

What's in a Name?

Britain was the first country in the world to build factories to manufacture products on an industrial scale. Factory is a shortened version of the word "manufactory," which comes from the word "manufacture."

This engraving shows metalworkers pouring hot molten iron into a mold at a foundry.

Flour Mill

One of the most dangerous factory jobs was working in a flour mill. Children as young as 6 years old often worked 10 hours a day grinding grain on huge millstones to turn it into flour. The children struggled to breathe because the air was full of grain dust.

Flour is the ground-up grain from cereal crops such as this wheat plant.

Flour Power

It was important for mill workers to make sure grain passed onto the millstones quickly. If they were too slow, the empty stones would grind together and create a spark. This action could create an enormous explosion because the air in the mill was full of flour dust. The mill workers also faced another danger—they could become caught in the machinery and be seriously injured.

Bread Recipes

During the Industrial Revolution, bread was the most important, and sometimes the only, food for many people. When made properly, it was tasty and nutritious. However, some bakers tried to make bread cheaply by mixing flour with other ingredients, such as chalk and plaster. Poor people could afford only this cheap bread, which damaged their health.

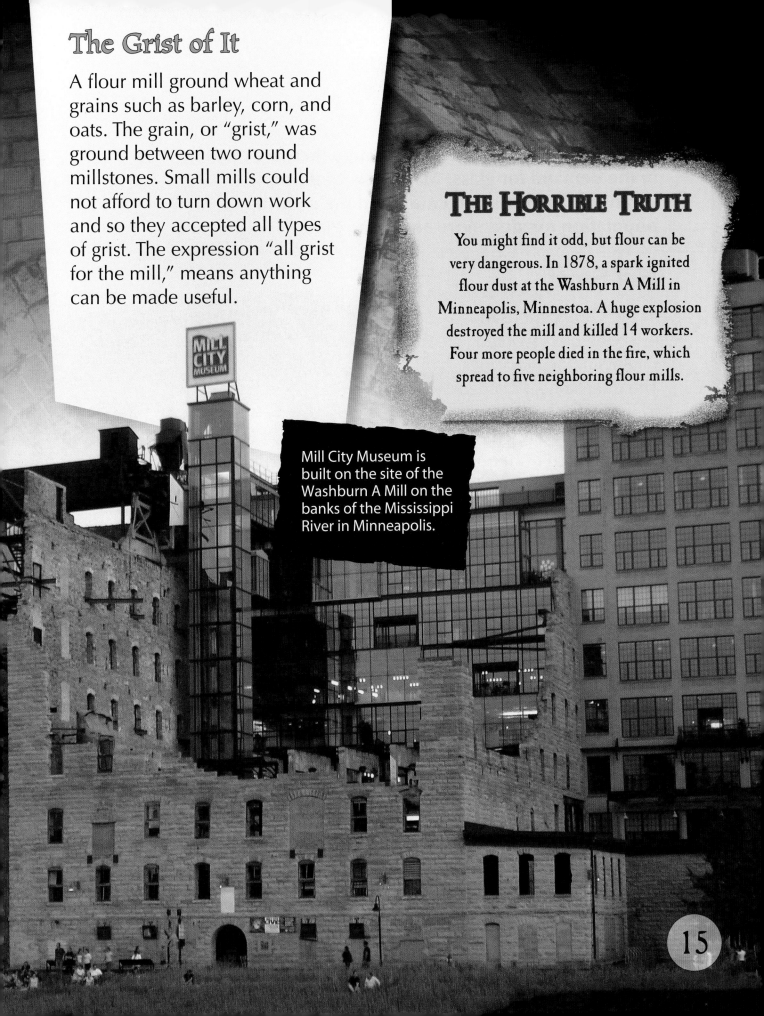

The Grist of It

A flour mill ground wheat and grains such as barley, corn, and oats. The grain, or "grist," was ground between two round millstones. Small mills could not afford to turn down work and so they accepted all types of grist. The expression "all grist for the mill," means anything can be made useful.

Mill City Museum is built on the site of the Washburn A Mill on the banks of the Mississippi River in Minneapolis.

THE HORRIBLE TRUTH

You might find it odd, but flour can be very dangerous. In 1878, a spark ignited flour dust at the Washburn A Mill in Minneapolis, Minnestoa. A huge explosion destroyed the mill and killed 14 workers. Four more people died in the fire, which spread to five neighboring flour mills.

Glassmaker

The Industrial Revolution saw a huge increase in the demand for glass. Many new buildings sprang up in towns and cities, and the growing population needed more and more glass.

Hot Stuff

In the 1800s, thousands of young boys worked in glassmaking factories. The intense heat needed to melt the glass meant that the poor glassmakers often suffered from burns and heat exhaustion. The workers were paid by each piece of glass they made, so they had to work very long hours, throughout the night and without breaks, to earn enough money.

These glassblowers worked at a factory in England. Working at a glassmaking factory was hard, hot work.

Blowing Glass

Bottles and decorative glass items were made by glass blowing. During the process, a piece of solid glass was heated until it was red hot. A long pipe was then pushed into the glass, through which the glassmaker blew to shape the molten glass. By repeatedly blowing, turning, and heating, the glass blower formed the desired shape.

Making Windows

During the Industrial Revolution, windows were made from sheets of glass. Glass workers fed molten glass through two rollers, and polished the sheet when the glass had cooled. Glassmakers wore thick gloves and protective clothes, but, despite this, they still were often badly cut.

Building a Palace

Crystal Palace housed the Great Exhibition of 1851, at which the latest inventions from the Industrial Revolution were displayed.

In 1851, the largest glass building ever made was built in Hyde Park in London, England. Thousands of sheets of glass were made for this amazing structure. The magnificent building was called the Crystal Palace, and it housed the latest inventions from all over the world. Sadly, the Crystal Palace burned down in 1936.

Matchstick Girls

In London, hundreds of women and young girls worked in factories during the Industrial Revolution, where they made matchboxes and filled them with matchsticks. Some even worked at home to add to their wages.

Meet the Girls

The women and girls who did this job became known as "matchstick girls." They slaved away with poor pay for 14 hours a day and even had to pay fines if they did not make enough matchsticks. They used extremely dangerous chemicals, such as white phosphorus, to make matches. This chemical caused health problems such as "phossy jaw."

Jaw Dropping

Women who suffered from phossy jaw had a toothache and swelling in their gums. Abscesses then developed that emitted a smelly discharge in the mouth. Eventually, the women became brain damaged and died unless their jaws were removed. The use of white phosphorus in matches was banned in Britain in 1910.

Many matchstick girls developed phossy jaw caused by the exposure to white phosphorus while making matches.

Matchstick girls packed hundreds of matches into matchboxes every day. It was a boring and dangerous job.

Strike a Light

In July 1888, a matchstick girl at the Bryant & May match factory in London was fired. The other workers in the factory were outraged. By the end of the day, 1,400 matchstick girls had walked out in protest at the factory's terrible working conditions and fines. Eventually, the factory owners improved working conditions for the matchstick girls.

Safety First

Phosphorus matches are dangerous because you can strike them against any surface to light the match. This can lead to burns and fires. Today, most matches are safety matches, which can only be lit by striking them against a special surface on the matchbox itself.

Metalworker

Metal was an important raw material during the Industrial Revolution. Many people worked as metalworkers in factories to extract metals from their ores and cast them into different shapes.

The cast iron bridge at Ironbridge near Telford in Shropshire, England, is a lasting monument to the Industrial Revolution.

In the Heat

Metals such as iron come from metal ores, which were processed in factories. Huge blast furnaces heated the rocks into molten ore, which separated the metal from the rock. Some workers constantly shoveled coal into the blast furnaces, while others forged the molten metal into different shapes. A job at the metalworks involved 12-hour shifts in the sweltering heat. Workers breathed in poisonous fumes, and had the constant fear that they might be horribly burned.

Different Kinds of Iron

The molten iron that comes from iron ore is called pig iron. In the late 1700s, this iron was modified to create a stronger wrought iron. Eventually, metalworkers came up with a way of making even stronger cast iron. This was the strongest iron developed during the Industrial Revolution, and it was used to make bridges, machines, and many other structures. Many of these strong structures can still be seen today.

Puddle Trouble

Metalworkers called "puddlers" did the most skilled and dangerous job in an iron foundry. They stirred the molten pig iron and added chemicals to increase the heat of the molten mixture. Finally, the puddlers drained the waste, called slag, and rolled the iron into huge balls ready for processing. All the time, they worked in incredible heat. They were constantly covered in sweat and breathed in toxic fumes from the molten metal mixture.

A job at the metalworks was tough. The puddler had one of the hardest jobs, working long shifts in unbearable heat.

"Iron Mad" John

Men who ran ironworks were called "iron masters." John Wilkinson was an iron master who funded the first iron bridge at Ironbridge in England. When he died, John Wilkinson was buried in an iron coffin, which is why he got his nickname— "Iron Mad" John.

Mule Piecer and Scavenger

Another dangerous factory job was working in a cotton mill. These factories contained huge machines called spinning mules, which never stopped working. Many cotton workers were crushed and injured by the moving parts of the machines.

Cotton was a very valuable raw material during the Industrial Revolution.

The girl working on the spinning mule is a piecer. The boy working under the machine is a scavenger.

Mule Piecer

The mule piecer worked on the spinning mule, which spun cotton into thread ready for weaving into cloth. The piecer had to stick broken pieces of cotton together while the spinning mule was still moving. Many mule piecers had their hands and fingers torn off by the moving parts of the machine.

Mule Scavenger

The mule scavenger gathered up all the pieces of cotton fluff that drifted under the machines. Scavengers were the youngest workers in the cotton mill—often children as young as 5 years old. Although they were small, scavengers still faced the risk of being crushed by the moving machinery.

Greedy Owners

Factory owners liked to employ children because they were small and nimble, which meant they could get under and between the spinning mules. The factory owners were only concerned with making money. The machines had no safety guards, and injuries were common.

A Tiring Day

Children working in a cotton mill walked to and from work every day. If they did something wrong, they could be fined or even beaten. If the children fell asleep at a machine, which many did after too many long hours of hard work, the poor young workers were dipped upside down in a tank of cold water.

This young boy worked as a mule scavenger in a cotton mill in Chattanooga, Tennessee.

THE HORRIBLE TRUTH

Working in the cotton mill was bad for the workers' health. Many workers had deformed legs, a condition that became known as being "knock kneed," and back deformities. Lung diseases were common because the workers constantly breathed in cotton dust.

Tanner

The tanner had one of the most disgusting jobs of all during the Industrial Revolution. It was the tanner's job to make animal hides into leather to make shoes, belts, and other products.

Tanners had to scrape the hides of dead animals, such as goats, sheep, and cows, to make into leather goods.

Terrible Job

The first step in the tanning process was to remove the hair and rotting flesh from the animal hide by soaking it in urine for a week. Then next part of the job was truly disgusting. The tanner mixed water with dogs' waste and dunked the hides in it. This removed the urine and softened the hide, now ready to be made into goods. Tanners were skilled workers, but they lived on the edges of society because they stank!

Tanners collected dog waste to soften leather hides.

Pure Finders

Of course, if the tannery was going to use dog, and sometimes pigeon, waste, then somebody had to collect it. This was a job for the pure finders. They would scour the streets for dog waste, collect it in a pail, and sell it to the tannery. The pure finders were the first ever pooper-scoopers!

Leather is used to make many different items, from boots to belts.

Children would collect pots of urine on street corners and take them to the tanner.

Urine Corner

In some towns, pots were placed on street corners so that people could urinate in them. Every now and again, a child would collect the pot and take it to the tanner. The urine might also be taken to the washerwoman, because the urine was also used to make "lant," a mixture used for cleaning clothes.

The Workhouse

The prize for the worst place to work has to go to the British workhouse and the US poorhouse. Many people, mainly orphans and the homeless, ended up in workhouses or poorhouses, where they lived and worked in horrible conditions.

Bread and Gruel

The British and US governments stated that if people were poor and had no work, they had to go into a workhouse or poorhouse. It was meant to be a last resort for the poor, and it was designed to be so unpleasant that people would do anything rather than go to one. Inside the institutes, families were split up, and people were fed only bread and watery soup, called gruel. The work was hard and punishments were extremely harsh.

The City College workhouse in Southampton, England, dates back to 1866.

People worked in silence at the Coldbath Fields workhouse in Clerkenwell, London.

House of Horror

Workhouses and poorhouses were overcrowded and rife with diseases. There, people did the jobs no one else wanted to do. Some people broke stones for building roads, while others made ropes for use in the shipbuilding industry.

THE HORRIBLE TRUTH

Grinding bones to make fertilizer was a common task in workhouses. In 1845, workers in Andover, England, were given bones to grind. Instead of grinding the bones, the starving workers began to eat them. The workhouse master had stolen the money meant for the workers' food, so they were starving.

27

Chapter Three On the Move

During the Industrial Revolution, wealthy countries such as the United States built transportation systems to get raw materials to factories. New canals and railroads linked the industrial centers with ports so that the finished goods could be shipped to other countries around the world.

Transporting Goods

Before the Industrial Revolution, the fastest way to travel was on horseback or by boat on rivers. Most people could not afford a horse, however, and the roads were in terrible condition—especially in the winter. Heavy goods could only be transported by river, if there was one close by, or on packhorses. Something had to be done to improve the transportation system.

People once had to pay a fee to use the road next to this toll house in Britain.

Building Turnpikes

Road builders started to build new stone roads in the 1700s. The roads were called "turnpikes" and people had to pay a fee to use them. Many people refused to pay to use the turnpikes. In the 1840s in Wales, a group of men dressed up as women destroyed the tollbooths for many turnpike roads. They were called the Rebecca Rioters because of the disguises they chose.

This statue is of Blind Jack Metcalf, one of the most prolific roadbuilders of the Industrial Revolution.

Blind Jack Metcalf

Jack Metcalf was blind from the age of 6, but that did not stop him from becoming the first professional road builder. He built hundreds of miles of road, including one across a bog that was built on rafts made of heather.

Canal Legger

Canal leggers had one of the most unglamorous jobs of the Industrial Revolution. They guided canal boats, called barges, through the narrow tunnels that made up the canal system. The barges were laden with heavy raw materials and many goods.

Canals were one of the most important transportation networks of the Industrial Revolution.

Mind the Gap

Out in the open, horses on towpaths pulled canal boats along the waterways. Tunnels were expensive to build, but were necessary to cross under high ground. To save money, the tunnels were made as narrow as possible—often only wide enough for the boat. Horses could not drag the boats through tunnels—this was the tiring job of the canal legger.

Later, canal tunnels were widened so that horses could pull the boats through them.

Walking on Walls

Two canal leggers lay on their backs on wooden planks that were laid on the boats. They then "walked" along the walls, guiding the boat through the narrow tunnel. This was backbreaking and dangerous work. Many leggers fell off the planks and were crushed to death by the boat.

Well Paid?

Canal workers were well paid because their work was so dangerous. Workers in the United States could earn as much as $200 per month, which was a huge amount of money for a laborer during the time of the Industrial Revolution. However, as the railroads developed and more goods were transported by train, canal workers earned less.

Leg Work

The people who worked on the barge would leg the boat along short tunnels, but some tunnels were as long as 3 miles (4.8 km). The barge workers tried to save money by legging through long tunnels themselves, without the help of a canal legger. However, professional leggers didn't like this and sometimes forced the barge workers into paying for the service.

On the Trains

The arrival of steam power and the railroad system opened up the land during the Industrial Revolution. People could travel between major cities on the railroads much more quickly than before. The railroads were vital for industrial countries. By 1900, there were more than one million railroad workers in the United States.

Firemen shoveled coal into the firebox of locomotives.

Fire Power

Steam engines needed coal for power, and one horrible job was that of the fireman—the person who shoveled coal into the firebox to power the engine. Another equally horrible job was the engine cleaner, who had to crawl inside the firebox to clean out all the soot. The cleaner also had to clean out the ashtrays, by climbing under the locomotives and scraping a long brush along the trays to get rid of the muck. The engine driver had the easiest job by far!

Pennsylvania Railroad Company

People did not earn a lot of money working on the railroads. When the Pennsylvania Railroad Company cut wages by 10 percent, the workers went on strike. The company brought in the state militia to keep the railroad running. This prompted a riot that caused $2 million worth of damage.

A Slow Start

Modern electric trains can start with the flick of a switch. Steam trains required a lot of work and effort to get them going. Early in the morning, several hours before the train was due to depart, a "lighter" started a fire to heat the boiler. Only then could the fireman start to shovel coal into the firebox, which heated water in the boiler to produce the steam.

Steam locomotives revolutionized transportation during the Industrial Revolution. People could cover long distances far more quickly by train than on horseback.

33

Navvy

Of all the horrible jobs involved in the sprawling transportation system, one of the hardest must have been the navvy. Navvies worked as part of a gang of laborers. It was their job to work the land, shifting hundreds of tons of earth to build canals, dig tunnels, and lay railroad tracks.

Navvies hammer railroad tracks into the ground in West Virginia. This photograph was taken around 1860.

Tools for the Job

The only tools navvies had were hand shovels and wheelbarrows. Sometimes, they used dangerous explosives to dig tunnels. Many were killed in the process. Navvies lived in dirty accommodations on site and were paid a small wage, along with meat and ale. If the navvies were sick, they were not paid anything at all.

Navvy Britain

At one point in Britain in the nineteenth century, 1 in every 100 workers was a navvy. Each shifted up to 20 tons (18 mt) of earth every day. There were few safety measures in place, so accidents were common. Many navvies died doing their job. If a navvy died, his wife might get $5 as a widow's pension, if she was lucky.

Drinking Ale

Navvies worked hard all day long and after they finished work they liked to enjoy a drink of ale. Sometimes navvies would drink for days on end. This was called "going on a randy." Many towns and communities feared the arrival of a gang of navvies because they would get drunk and misbehave. Only the innkeeper was happy, because the navvies spent their money in his inn.

Dynamite made building tunnels much quicker, but many navvies died in the explosions.

John Henry

John Henry was a famous navvy who worked in West Virginia. He hammered drills into rocks to make holes for explosives. He worked so quickly that, one day, he raced a steam hammer to see which was quicker. Henry won the race, but then died of exhaustion!

Chapter Four
At Your Service!

During the Industrial Revolution, wealthy people got richer, while the poor grew poorer. Many poor people became servants in the houses of the rich. They were often treated as slaves and had horrible jobs.

Dead-end Jobs

Large houses might employ a lot of people to do many different jobs. At the lower end of the servant scale, the boot boys cleaned shoes and carried out other minor tasks. Scullery maids performed simple cooking and cleaning jobs.

Top Jobs

Important roles for male servants were as butlers—who were in charge of the wine, silverware, and other servants—and as valets, who organized their masters' clothes. Important female roles included the nanny, who educated and cared for the younger children, and the housekeeper, who was in charge of food and the housemaids.

The British artist William Hogarth painted this picture of his servants in the mid 1700s.

During the Industrial Revolution, there were few household appliances. Electric irons, toasters, and vacuum cleaners became available only in the twentieth century. As a result, most chores had to be done by hand. If the work was not completed properly, servants might be dismissed without a reference. It was then almost impossible to find work.

Serves You Right

Servants were expected to speak only when they were spoken to, and had to lower their eyes when one of their masters or mistresses walked past. When leaving a room, the servant was expected to walk backward as a sign of respect. There was also a strict hierarchy of servants, and servants were expected to be polite to any senior workers.

Electric irons were not available in the Industrial Revolution. Housemaids had to heat an iron, such as this one, on a stove, and then iron clothes. It took a long time!

Housemaid

Wealthy, prosperous households during the Industrial Revolution had an army of maids to attend to all the household chores. They cleaned, cooked, cared for children, and did the ironing and the laundry.

A team of servants ran the huge houses of the wealthy during the Industrial Revolution.

Slave Service

Maids were often treated like slaves and were paid very little. They had only one meal a day and slept in a cramped room with all the other housemaids. Many housemaids suffered from "housemaid's knee"—an inflammation of the knee that resulted from spending hours scrubbing floors on their hands and knees.

A Long Day

A typical day for a maid might start at 5 a.m. Maids washed and dressed, and then cleaned and laid the fires. The day included preparing, serving, and clearing up after three meals. Endless tasks such as polishing, ironing, dusting, and scrubbing were carried out. Often the maid went to bed only after the master of the house, who might stay up past midnight. Her day would start again 5 hours later!

Luck of the Master

The quality of life for a maid depended on her master. Unlucky maids might have to sleep in the kitchen or even in a cupboard. A maid had to be as quiet as possible. If she dropped and broke something, she had to pay for it out of her small wage. Maids were not allowed to laugh, and had to be ready to work or fetch something at a moment's notice.

Housemaids did many different jobs. Clothes had to be washed on a washboard like this one.

Testing Times

The master or mistress sometimes placed dirt in awkward places to test a maid's thoroughness. Money was often left under a carpet to test her honesty, too. The behavior of the maid was constantly scrutinized, and if she made any small mistake, it could lead to her dismissal.

Rat Catcher

Rats were common pests during the Industrial Revolution because of the lack of clean water in the ever-expanding towns and cities. Rats carried horrible diseases, so wealthy households employed rat catchers to get rid of the troublesome rodents.

Jack Black was rat catcher to Queen Victoria.

Chemical Attraction

Rat catchers mixed dangerous chemicals to create poisons to kill the rodent pests. Sometimes, they caught live rats, which they sold to landlords for dog fights, a popular sport in taverns. The rat catchers covered their hands in sweet-smelling oil, which attracted the rats. Catching live rats was dangerous because the rat catchers might be bitten and catch not only the rats, but nasty diseases, too.

Jack Black

Jack Black was a famous rat catcher. Jack nearly died of disease on several occasions after being bitten, and his face and body were badly scarred. Jack Black was a fearsome rat catcher, sometimes he even ate rats!

Posh Pets

Jack Black collected strangely colored rats and sold them to rich ladies, who kept them as pets. The famous writer Beatrix Potter is said to have bought a rat from Jack Black.

Rats are a common cause of disease, so rat catching was big business during the Industrial Revolution.

Rat Pit

Jimmy Shaw was a tavern owner and rat catcher in nineteenth-century London. His tavern had a rat-baiting pit where dogs were made to fight rats. Shaw's children helped out during the fights, and their fingers were black and scarred from rat bites. Sometimes a brave, or perhaps crazy, man would get into the pit and fight the rats himself. He killed them by biting off their heads—gross!

Rat baiting was a popular sport in taverns.

41

Chimney Sweep

Chimney sweeps, or climbing boys, had one of the dirtiest jobs of the Industrial Revolution. They crawled up tiny channels to brush poisonous soot out of the chimneys.

Fit for the Job

The youngest climbing boys were 5 or 6 years old. The master sweeps preferred younger children because they were small enough to climb the narrowest chimneys. Sometimes, the chimneys were as narrow as 9 square inches (58 sq cm).

Most climbing boys were very young because they were small enough to fit up the narrow chimneys.

Hard Work

Sweeping out chimneys was unhealthy and very dangerous. The sweeps had sore feet and skinned knees and elbows. They constantly breathed in poisonous soot, and many got lung cancer as a result. The young sweeps also faced being burned if the chimney was hot, becoming stuck up the chimney, and suffocating in its poisonous fumes.

Sweep's Life

Many chimney sweeps came from the workhouse. They served an apprenticeship under the master sweep. The master sweep made sure that the apprentice washed at least once a week—it was a filthy job.

THE HORRIBLE TRUTH

The master would harden a new sweep's skin by exposing his knees and elbows to heat and rubbing in salty water. Ouch! If a master thought a sweep was too slow, he would send another boy up the chimney after him with a pin, to prick his feet and bottom to hurry him along.

The End of the Industrial Revolution

The changes that took place during the Industrial Revolution happened over many years, starting in the late 1700s and ending in the early 1900s.

Huge Change

The Industrial Revolution was a time of tremendous growth and prosperity in Britain, the United States, and other western countries. Before this time, most people worked the land, growing crops and raising livestock on small farms and allotments. The Industrial Revolution saw many new inventions, from steam engines and electric motors to spinning mules and sewing machines. As a result, many people moved from the country to city centers to work in factories. The landscape changed, too, with bridges, canals, and railroads crisscrossing the land.

A driver and his passengers enjoy a ride in a Model T Ford. The mass production of automobiles was one of the last great advances of the Industrial Revolution.

A Hard Life

The Industrial Revolution made many people very rich, but life was hard for ordinary people working in the coal mines and factories. The working day often lasted 12 hours or more—often in terrible conditions—with strict rules and very little pay. Many families were so poor that they had to send their children out to work, and they were forced to do dangerous jobs instead of going to school.

End of an Era

In many ways, the Industrial Revolution never really ended. Today, we see many amazing new inventions all the time, from electric cars to touchscreen computers. Some people suggest that the terrible world wars of the twentieth century marked the end of the Industrial Revolution. During these wars, many machines were invented, such as tanks, machine guns, and jet engines, although many of them ended lives rather than improved them.

The Computer Revolution

The invention of computers and the Internet has been called the "new industrial revolution." The machines that powered the original Industrial Revolution replaced manual labor and made factories produce more goods more quickly. Computers are machines that help us by storing, accessing, and processing information more quickly than before. They speed up everyday tasks such as shopping on the Internet and communicating by email.

New inventions, such as smartphones with digital cameras, are part of the new computer revolution that is changing our lives.

Glossary

blast furnaces extremely hot fires used to extract metals from their ores

canal legger a worker who pushed canal barges through narrow tunnels by walking along the walls of the tunnel

caustic soda a corrosive chemical, also known as lye or sodium hydroxide

coke a powdery form of coal used to extract metals from their ores

corfs coal carts

getters coal miners who dug coal at the coalface

grist grain such as barley, corn, oats, and wheat meant for grinding

hurrier a coal miner who moved cartloads of coal to the surface of the mine

millstones huge flat stones that were used to grind grain into flour at a flourmill

mule piecer a worker who stuck broken pieces of cotton on the spinning mule

mule scavenger a worker who collected scraps of cotton fluff at the cotton mill

navvy a worker who dug up the land to build canals, dig tunnels, and lay railroad tracks

ore rock that contains metals

phossy jaw a disease caused by breathing in a chemical element called white phosphorus

poorhouse a place where poor and homeless people were sent to work during the Industrial Revolution

puddlers metalworkers who stirred molten iron in a blast furnace

pure finders people who collected dogs' waste and sold it to a tannery to make leather

putters coal miners who took the coal to the surface

Queen Victoria queen of Great Britain who ruled for much of the nineteenth century

spinning mule a machine that spins cotton into thread ready for weaving into cloth

steam engines engines that use steam to drive pistons to produce power

tanner a worker who processed animal hides into leather

thruster a hurrier who pushed cartloads of coal with their heads

trapper a coal worker who opened and closed trap doors in the mines to let the coal trucks through

turnpike a stone road that people had to pay to use

workhouse a place where poor and homeless people were sent to work during the Industrial Revolution

For More Information

Books

Malam, John. *The Danger Zone: Avoid Working in a Victorian Mill*. Brighton, England: Book House, 2007.

Meinking, Mary. *The Development of U.S. Industry: 1870 to 1900*. Ann Arbor, MI: Cherry Lake Publishing, 2012.

Robinson, Tony. *The Worst Children's Jobs in History*. London, England: Macmillan Children's Books, 2005.

Websites

This website has lots of links to activities, animations, and games to help you learn more about the Industrial Revolution:
www.wartgames.com/themes/industrialrevolution.html

Find out more about the role of women in the industrial revolution at:
www.gilderlehrman.org/history-by-era/jackson-lincoln/essays/women-and-early-industrial-revolution-united-states

The History Learning Site has lots of interesting links about life during the Industrial Revolution:
www.historylearningsite.co.uk/indrevo.htm

Publisher's note to educators and parents: Our editors have carefully reviewed these websites to ensure that they are suitable for students. Many websites change frequently, however, and we cannot guarantee that a site's future contents will continue to meet our high standards of quality and educational value. Be advised that students should be closely supervised whenever they access the Internet.

Index